HOW TO WRITE A SUCCESSFUL CV

JOANNA GUTMANN established her training consultancy ten years ago, concentrating on interpersonal office skills. She runs a variety of courses throughout the country covering a broad range of subjects, from presentation and assertiveness skills to communication skills, telephone techniques and business letter and report writing.

Joanna is experienced in helping people present themselves in a professional manner, whilst retaining their individual character.

Overcoming Common Problems Series

For a full list of titles please contact
Sheldon Press, Marylebone Road, London NW1 4DU

The Assertiveness Workbook
A plan for busy women
JOANNA GUTMANN

Beating the Comfort Trap
DR WINDY DRYDEN AND JACK GORDON

Birth Over Thirty Five
SHEILA KITZINGER

Body Language
How to read others' thoughts by their gestures
ALLAN PEASE

Body Language in Relationships
DAVID COHEN

Calm Down
How to cope with frustration and anger
DR PAUL HAUCK

Cancer – A Family Affair
NEVILLE SHONE

Comfort for Depression
JANET HORWOOD

Coping Successfully with Hayfever
DR ROBERT YOUNGSON

Coping Successfully with Migraine
SUE DYSON

Coping Successfully with Pain
NEVILLE SHONE

Coping Successfully with PMS
KAREN EVENNETT

Coping Successfully with Panic Attacks
SHIRLEY TRICKETT

Coping Successfully with Prostate Problems
ROSY REYNOLDS

Coping Successfully with Your Hyperactive Child
DR PAUL CARSON

Coping Successfully with Your Irritable Bowel
ROSEMARY NICOL

Coping Successfully with Your Second Child
FIONA MARSHALL

Coping with Anxiety and Depression
SHIRLEY TRICKETT

Coping with Blushing
DR ROBERT EDELMANN

Coping with Bronchitis and Emphysema
DR TOM SMITH

Coping with Candida
SHIRLEY TRICKETT

Coping with Chronic Fatigue
TRUDIE CHALDER

Coping with Cot Death
SARAH MURPHY

Coping with Crushes
ANITA NAIK

Coping with Cystitis
CAROLINE CLAYTON

Coping with Depression and Elation
DR PATRICK McKEON

Coping with Postnatal Depression
FIONA MARSHALL

Coping with Psoriasis
PROFESSOR RONALD MARKS

Coping with Schizophrenia
DR STEVEN JONES AND DR FRANK TALLIS

Coping with Strokes
DR TOM SMITH

Coping with Suicide
DR DONALD SCOTT

Coping with Thyroid Problems
DR JOAN GOMEZ

Coping with Thrush
CAROLINE CLAYTON

Curing Arthritis Exercise Book
MARGARET HILLS AND JANET HORWOOD

Curing Arthritis Diet Book
MARGARET HILLS

Curing Arthritis – The Drug-Free Way
MARGARET HILLS

Overcoming Common Problems Series

Curing Arthritis
More ways to a drug-free life
MARGARET HILLS

Curing Illness – The Drug-Free Way
MARGARET HILLS

Depression
DR PAUL HAUCK

Divorce and Separation
Every woman's guide to a new life
ANGELA WILLANS

Don't Blame Me!
How to stop blaming yourself and other people
TONY GOUGH

Everything Parents Should Know About Drugs
SARAH LAWSON

Family First Aid and Emergency Handbook
DR ANDREW STANWAY

Getting Along with People
DIANNE DOUBTFIRE

Getting the Best for Your Bad Back
DR ANTHONY CAMPBELL

Good Stress Guide, The
MARY HARTLEY

Heart Attacks – Prevent and Survive
DR TOM SMITH

Helping Children Cope with Bullying
SARAH LAWSON

Helping Children Cope with Divorce
ROSEMARY WELLS

Helping Children Cope with Grief
ROSEMARY WELLS

Hold Your Head Up High
DR PAUL HAUCK

How to Be Your Own Best Friend
DR PAUL HAUCK

How to Cope when the Going Gets Tough
DR WINDY DRYDEN AND JACK GORDON

How to Cope with Bulimia
DR JOAN GOMEZ

How to Cope with Difficult People
ALAN HOUEL WITH CHRISTIAN GODEFROY

How to Cope with Splitting Up
VERA PEIFFER

How to Cope with Stress
DR PETER TYRER

How to Cope with your Child's Allergies
DR PAUL CARSON

How to Do What You Want to Do
DR PAUL HAUCK

How to Improve Your Confidence
DR KENNETH HAMBLY

How to Interview and Be Interviewed
MICHELE BROWN AND GYLES BRANDRETH

How to Keep Your Cholesterol in Check
DR ROBERT POVEY

How to Love and Be Loved
DR PAUL HAUCK

How to Pass Your Driving Test
DONALD RIDLAND

How to Stand up for Yourself
DR PAUL HAUCK

How to Start a Conversation and Make Friends
DON GABOR

How to Stop Smoking
GEORGE TARGET

How to Stop Worrying
DR FRANK TALLIS

How to Survive Your Teenagers
SHEILA DAINOW

How to Untangle Your Emotional Knots
DR WINDY DRYDEN AND JACK GORDON

How to Write a Successful CV
JOANNA GUTMANN

Hysterectomy
SUZIE HAYMAN

Is HRT Right for You?
DR ANNE MACGREGOR

The Incredible Sulk
DR WINDY DRYDEN

The Irritable Bowel Diet Book
ROSEMARY NICOL

The Irritable Bowel Stress Book
ROSEMARY NICOL

Overcoming Common Problems Series

Jealousy
DR PAUL HAUCK

Learning to Live with Multiple Sclerosis
DR ROBERT POVEY, ROBIN DOWIE AND GILLIAN PRETT

Living Through Personal Crisis
ANN KAISER STEARNS

Living with Asthma
DR ROBERT YOUNGSON

Living with Diabetes
DR JOAN GOMEZ

Living with Grief
DR TONY LAKE

Living with High Blood Pressure
DR TOM SMITH

Making the Most of Loving
GILL COX AND SHEILA DAINOW

Making the Most of Yourself
GILL COX AND SHEILA DAINOW

Menopause
RAEWYN MACKENZIE

Migraine Diet Book, The
SUE DYSON

Motor Neurone Disease – A Family Affair
DR DAVID OLIVER

The Nervous Person's Companion
DR KENNETH HAMBLY

Overcoming Guilt
DR WINDY DRYDEN

Overcoming Stress
DR VERNON COLEMAN

The Parkinson's Disease Handbook
DR RICHARD GODWIN-AUSTEN

Sleep Like a Dream – The Drug-Free Way
ROSEMARY NICOL

Subfertility Handbook, The
VIRGINIA IRONSIDE AND SARAH BIGGS

Talking About Anorexia
How to cope with life without starving
MAROUSHKA MONRO

Talking About Miscarriage
SARAH MURPHY

Ten Steps to Positive Living
DR WINDY DRYDEN

Think Your Way to Happiness
DR WINDY DRYDEN AND JACK GORDON

Understanding Obsessions and Compulsions
A self-help manual
DR FRANK TALLIS

Understanding Your Personality
Myers-Briggs and more
PATRICIA HEDGES

A Weight Off Your Mind
How to stop worrying about your body size
SUE DYSON

When your Child Comes Out
ANNE LOVELL

You and Your Varicose Veins
DR PATRICIA GILBERT

Overcoming Common Problems

HOW TO WRITE A SUCCESSFUL CV

Joanna Gutmann

First published in Great Britain in 1995 by
Sheldon Press, SPCK, Marylebone Road, London NW1 4DU

Second impression 1996

British Library Cataloguing-in-Publication Data
A catalogue record for this book is available from the British Library

ISBN 0–85969–693–6

Photoset by Deltatype Ltd, Ellesmere Port, Cheshire
Printed in Great Britain by Biddles Ltd, Guildford and King's Lynn

Contents

Introduction

A curriculum vitae, or CV, is the advertisement by which you sell yourself. If it is poorly photocopied, badly laid out and full of mistakes it will tell a potential employer nothing that will make him want to employ you. However, if it is crisp, tidy, and easy on the eye it will encourage a second look.

Your CV will only get a few minutes attention so it must give all the right signals. It should be a brief, factual account of your experience and qualifications. All other information should be in the covering letter or saved for the interview. It is a business document, and like all the best business documents should be completely professional, but showing a little of the person who has written it.

This workbook will guide you in a simple and practical way through the preparation of a professional, businesslike CV. By the end of the book you will have a full draft of your CV, ready to be typed up and sent.

The Five Most Common Mistakes

1 Poor photocopying. Examples include CVs which are not straight on the page, are smudged, spotted, or are a faded 'copy of a copy'.
2 Typing, grammatical, and spelling mistakes.
3 Unappealing layout with no continuity of style in either layout or wording (or both).
4 Disorganized – information in different places and sometimes duplicated, dates out of order, relevant information not clearly visible.
5 Too long – more than two pages.

If you can avoid these mistakes, you will already be ahead of much of the competition – and that is before anyone has looked at your experience and qualifications!

What should a CV look like?

Your CV should look reasonably traditional, professional and uncluttered, and should be a maximum of two pages long. Imagine ploughing through a pile of CVs on your desk. It will be the front page that catches your eye and makes you take the trouble to glance at the second page. Few employers will bother to read through more, and thus it is vital to get everything you want the employer to see on these two pages. This does not mean cramming the words in and using a small typeface. Rather, it is important to concentrate on what it is about your employment history and qualifications that will make your CV worth putting on the 'possible' pile.

Do not fall into the trap of trying to catch the eye of the recruiter by using gimmicks with layout, paper colour, illustrations, etc. Remember, although there is a chance that your CV might be read by someone with a sense of humour similar to yours, there is a far greater chance that you will look flippant and that your approach will irritate the reader, who has many CVs to study and wants to find the information they expect, where they expect it. Most recruiters want to employ skilled and talented people who will fit into the existing workforce – your CV needs to fit the mould.

You should stick to A4 paper, typed on one side, using a popular typeface. With the availability of desktop publishing and a wide variety of fonts (typefaces) on even basic word processors, it is tempting to overdo the layout of your CV, with the result that it looks too published and insufficiently human. The section on presentation and layout will give you further guidance.

A CV for each application?

Ideally, yes! It is only a matter of the way you present the information, but you can make significant changes to the way in which you are viewed by simply changing the way you present the information.

For example, an administrator who is applying for a more senior but similar post will emphasize the knowledge and skills necessary to be effective in this type of work. If, however, she is applying for an office management post, the emphasis will be on the interpersonal aspects of each post she has held.

If you do not have access to wordprocessing or desktop publishing facilities, you may have no choice but to type one CV and send a fresh photocopy each time. If this is the case, identify the skills and experience that will make you most attractive in the job market and present a rounded view, emphasizing different skills and experience gained from each job.

Using the Workbook

The workbook is arranged to correspond to the main sections of a CV. As you read through it, consider how you are going to phrase your experience so that the most important facts are the ones that catch the eye of the employer.

The first two sections are for everyone. The third section, on employment history, is split into seven parts, the first for everyone, followed by subsidiary sections:

- for those who are currently in work and looking for a change or career progression;
- for those who want to change direction completely;
- for those who are currently unemployed;
- for school, college or university leavers. This section may also benefit anyone who is looking for a change of direction;
- for people looking to return to work after a career break;
- a general section on presenting your previous employment.

The remainder, with sections on education/qualifications, personal details, pastimes, layout and so on, is relevant to all CVs.

At the end of each section is a box for you to use to outline that particular part of your CV. As you read through each section, scribble notes on points that apply to you or ways in which you can outline your experience. When you have finished a section, start to rough out what you want to say in that part of your CV. When you are happy with it, write it out in the box provided.

At the end of the book, you can type out the contents of each box and there will be your CV, ready to be proof read, tidied up and sent!

Before you begin

Begin by identifying what it is about your career to date that makes you ready and right for the next move. This will show you the strand that should run through your CV; your qualifications and experience should be seen to pave the path to the obvious next step – the job you are applying for.

It will help to spend some time thinking positively about your skills and what you can bring to a job. Try not to write your CV when you are feeling down as your mood will come over in the tone of your sentences.

Exercise: think positively!

You must believe in yourself before you can begin to convince an employer that you are worth believing in.

Spend a few minutes thinking about your employment history, academic qualifications and any other experience or factors that make *you* right for the job (or type of job) you want to apply for.

Note down some key words below to help get you in the right frame of mind. You are not trying to write a CV at this stage, not even trying to write sentences. Just brainstorm, focusing on words and/or ideas which describe your strengths – the points you will want to bring to the forefront when you get down to the serious work.

Academic qualifications

____

____

____

Employment history

Other factors

1
Style and format

Although there is nothing to stop you giving the information about yourself in any style you wish, bear in mind the needs and interests of the employer. He or she will have tens, and quite possibly hundreds, of CVs to look through, and will naturally be drawn to the ones that are simple to read and easy on the eye. Although an employer may not want a 'yes-man', he is usually looking for someone who is reasonably traditional and will fit the mould – slot into the existing structures and conform.

A **creative** CV, the polite term for a gimmicky one, should only be used if you are applying for a creative job in a creative company. Even if it looks unusual, make sure that the information given still complies with the general principles of a CV. If you are using bright paper or a highly stylized typeface, look at it critically and see whether it is easy to read. Even the most futuristically inclined recruiter will not want to strain his eyes.

The two most common styles of CV are the **chronological** and **functional**, and these are explained below. Both start off with your personal details: name, address and telephone number, followed by employment history, qualifications, education, and so on. The difference is in the style of describing employment history.

The Chronological CV

This is the most common format for a CV, with employment history listed job by job, starting with the current or most recent. The headings within employment history should be the job title and company name, with responsibilities/accomplishments outlined for each.

This style makes your career pattern clear, highlighting the way in which your career has developed and emphasizing continuity of employment. It should be used when your job history shows continuing professional development, and it is ideal when the job you are applying for is a natural next step for you.

DAVID HENDERSON
14 Bath Road
Chapplewick
Bath, Avon

EMPLOYMENT HISTORY

1989-present	**INVESTMENT MANAGER** **Bantham Longstaff & Co, Bristol** Responsible for portfolios totalling £8.5m, invested mainly through the London Stock Exchange and in Unit and Investment Trusts. Growth in these portfolios has averaged 18% pa over the last four years. Liaison with private clients and corporate representatives. Management responsibility for attainment of targets by self and three Investment Assistants.
1984–1989	**PARTNERS ASSISTANT** **Haskins, Smith & Allen, London** Promoted from Clerk in 1987, responsibilities included administration of portfolios for corporate clients, presenting research information on British, European and North American companies and liaison with clients' investment staff.

This style also has one major advantage – it is the style that most employers are used to and are comfortable with.

Rules

- Start with your current or most recent post and work backwards.
- Only list the last four or five posts; summarize your employment before that under a heading such as 'Early Career'.
- Give most detail for your current post and reduce the amount as you work backwards. Keep the job you are applying for in mind and emphasize the points that support your application.
- For each post, outline your responsibilities and achievements and demonstrate your competence to do the work at that level. Do not worry about lesser responsibilities and routine tasks; these will be assumed and you can always fill in details at the interview.

An example of a chronological CV is shown on page 8, and a functional CV for the same person follows later in this section.

The Functional CV

The functional CV is laid out with your achievements and strengths in different areas grouped together, irrespective of where and when you have gained each. Obviously, the emphasis is lead by the requirements of the job you are applying for.

Although the job titles and employers are sometimes left off completely, it is preferable to give them as a list at the end of employment history. Most employers are interested in where you have worked and the posts you have held.

This style has the advantage of being very flexible and drawing attention away from career changes, periods away from work or where your employment history is patchy. If the employer is obviously looking for skills or experience that you have but do not demonstrate in your current job, it is a way of putting these first. It also avoids repetition where you have had several similar jobs.

DAVID HENDERSON
14 Bath Road
Chapplewick
Bath, Avon

EMPLOYMENT HISTORY

Portfolio Management

- Responsible for portfolios totalling £8.5m.
- Achieved actual growth of 18% over past four years.
- Experience of investment in London, Europe and North America.

Client Liaison

- Experience of dealing with clients with a broad range of understanding and experience of investment.
- Skilled at presenting complicated and detailed information in a simple and clear manner.
- Flexible and relaxed communication style, but with no loss of professionalism and accuracy of detail.

Management Skills

- Line responsibility for three investment assistants.
- Skilled team leader.
- Contributing member of quality assurance group.

Administration

- Experienced in maintaining accurate records.

Rules

- Select broad headings for your most relevant areas of expertise; stick to a maximum of five and quite possibly less.
- Under each, list your strengths and/or achievements in that area (usually with bullets).
- Do not show at which company (or in which leisure pursuit) you have demonstrated the strengths, although you will almost certainly be asked to substantiate your claims at interview.
- Follow the section with a list of your posts (date, title and company).
- The functional CV on page 10 is again for the investment manager shown before.

Before moving on, you should decide whether to opt for a chronological or functional CV. List the pros and cons of each style *for you*, and choose whichever is the most suitable for your experience.

Note: In some sections of the book the boxes for you to complete will suit either style. Where there is a choice, you need only complete the one for your chosen style. If you have decided to use a **functional CV**, you should complete the boxes in the relevant 'Employment History' sections and then amalgamate the information into one outline.

Whether you opt for a chronological or functional style, there are some rules which are vital:

Stick to one style

This applies to grammar and layout. Do not describe one job with bullets and the next with a paragraph of text. Similarly, avoid outlining your responsibilities in one post, and your achievements for another. Decide on the approach that best suits the most important part of your CV (probably your most recent or current job) and apply that to all.

Use the first person . . .

Always use 'I', not your first name. For example 'I was responsible for a team of . . .', not 'Jane was responsible for a team of . . .'

Or possibly no person

'Was responsible for a team of . . . .' 'I' is implied throughout a CV and so can be deemed unnecessary. It comes down to a matter of personal taste, but whether you use first or no person, stick to the same style throughout.

Put the most recent/relevant first

If you have chosen to prepare a **chronological** CV, start your employment history with the most recent job, and qualifications with the last and presumably most important, working backwards thereafter. If you prefer a **functional** CV, begin both employment history and qualifications with the most relevant (for the job you are applying for) and work backwards, this time in order of relevance.

Don't tell – show

Wherever possible, show your skills by example. For example, avoid vague terms such as 'good with people'. Instead, give the evidence: 'Supervised team of customer account clerks, dealing with around 100 queries per day. Dealt directly with customer complaints.'

Use active terms

Avoid the dull wordiness, e.g. 'My work involved the setting up and operation of a centralized filing department and computer-based information service.' Instead use a more personal and active style: 'I developed and managed a centralized filing department and built up a computer-based information service for use by 1750 employees.'

Other examples of passive words to avoid and active versions include:

Avoid	Use
completion of	completed
implementation of	implemented
provision of	provided
supervision of	supervised
training of	trained

Other useful active words include:

arranged	devised	organized
assisted	evaluated	oversaw
audited	examined	planned
built	expanded	presented
completed	identified	produced
consolidated	implemented	reviewed
controlled	improved	solved
co-ordinated	increased	studied
created	instructed	supervised
delivered	invented	translated
designed	maintained	trained
developed	operated	undertook

Ordering the Sections

The only section that has to be in a particular place is your name, address and telephone number. After that:

Career summary

If you wish to use one, put it next. It usually does not have a heading although if you want to head it, 'Career Summary' or 'Profile' are the two most common terms.

Employment history and qualifications/education

It is a matter of personal choice which of these two sections should be first. You should be governed by the length of your working history. If you have been working for less than three or four years, put your qualifications first – they will still be directly relevant to how employable you appear. After that time, your experience is likely to be more important and therefore this section should go first. Either way, make sure that your current or most recent job appears on the front page.

Other information

These are the miscellaneous details such as age, driving licence, etc. that can be grouped together under one heading.

Hobbies and pastimes

Although relating to your leisure time, these can say positive things about you. If you do little of interest or lack space on your CV, it can be left out, although you should be prepared to answer the question at interview.

All of these sections are covered in detail in the following pages.

2

Personal details

Some people give so much information in this section that they only just stop short of their credit card number. The only things that *must* be given are the following.

Name

Give your first name and surname, not initials. It is not necessary to give your title, although you may wish to if it is not clear from your name whether you are male or female. If you do so, you should put it in brackets after your name, e.g., Robin Jackson (Mrs). You should give the name you are known by, e.g., Jacqueline Harris. If you use your middle name, type it as J. Sarah Harris or alternatively, type it as Sarah Harris and under 'Other Information' put 'Full name: Jacqueline Sarah Harris'.

Address

You should give a full postal address. You may feel that your current employer's address adds stature (if it is suitably impressive and relevant), however, some employers will see it as indicating that you have been asked to leave and been given time to find alternative employment. Obviously, you should only give a company address if you are happy for letters to be sent there, and it is preferable to give your home address; employers expect this and it avoids sending an unsuitable message about your reasons for searching for work.

Telephone number

Give an office number only if you are able to receive calls and talk freely. If you do not want to be telephoned at work, give a home number only and say if it will only be answered in the evenings. Always give the STD code for any number.

Your name, primarily, and your address/telephone number form the heading of your CV and should be displayed as such.

Use bold type and a larger typeface for your name. Nothing in the remainder of the document should be larger.

Optional Extras

Many people also give details such as date of birth, marital status (and children), nationality, driving licence, etc., as part of this first section.

The disadvantage of this is that it takes up a great deal of space, out of all proportion with the relevance of the information. It also is visually less attractive and often means that important facts, such as current or most recent job, are relegated to the second page. It is preferable to put other personal details under 'Other Information' if you want to give the details at all, and they are dealt with under that chapter in this book.

Career Summary

If your qualifications are long ago, or poor in relation to the job you hold now, you should draw the employer's attention to the positive aspects of your experience. One way of doing this is through a career summary. Equally, if your experience is wide-ranging, a career summary will emphasize the experience which is most relevant.

Think of your career summary as a slogan, albeit a longer one than sells washing powder or cars. It should be one (or at most, two) sentences long and should identify the key benefits to be gained by employing you.

Before you write anything, read through the advertisement or job description and identify the one or two most important points. Use your summary to show your experience in these areas. This way, the most important features of your experience will be the ones the employer has identified as important to his company.

If you are writing a speculative CV, either keep the summary general or tailor it to suit the company you are sending it to. Make sure that you give information that is relevant to your next job, although obviously based on your current one. In other words, tailor it. For example:

A twenty-four-year-old car salesman with seven years' experience, spread over three companies, could phrase a career summary in any of the following ways, depending on the job he was applying for and/or the market he wanted to move into:

A sales executive with seven years' experience of . . .

- the motor trade (*general*);
- handling top-of-the-range car sales to private and executive company buyers (*e.g., applying for a job with Jaguar*);
- dealing with fleet buyers in companies of all sizes (*e.g., applying for a job with a garage that is setting up a company sales division*);
- private and company sales in the motor industry, now leading a dynamic sales team (*if applying for a first- or second-line management position*);
- dealing directly with company buyers and the general public at all levels (*e.g., applying for a job outside the motor industry*).

A career summary is by no means essential and is not particularly common. If you do want to include one, type in a slightly larger typeface, in bold type or centred to give emphasis. Do not type it in upper case; sentences in capital letters are difficult to read. Unless you feel a career summary will serve a particular purpose, it is best to omit it completely.

A photograph?

Do not send in a photograph unless specifically asked to do so. When they are requested, it is usually to help an interviewer recall each candidate after meeting with many in a day (not to check up on your appearance!).

Unless there are other instructions, glue it neatly to your CV (paperclips are not reliable and catch other papers).

Write a successful CV – personal details

Before you move on to the next chapter, complete the box below, filling in the sections as you would like them to appear on your CV.

Name ______________________________

Address ______________________________

____

____

Telephone

If you feel you must add in other personal details, note these:

____

____

____

____

____

____

Write a successful CV – career summary

This is optional. Only write one if you feel it will serve a useful purpose.

Checklist

Have you:

- ☐ Used your full first name (e.g., Elizabeth, not Liz)?
- ☐ Given the address you would like used for correspondence?
- ☐ Remembered to give the STD code with your telephone number?
- ☐ Only given additional personal details if you are sure they fulfil a specific purpose?
- ☐ Kept your career summary brief, positive and relevant (if you have chosen to use one)?

3
Employment history

This section is in seven parts; first, this general introduction, then five specific sections for those who are:

- currently **employed** and looking to move on;
- employed and looking for a **change of career**;
- **unemployed**;
- **school, college, or university leavers**;
- returning after a **career break**.

The final part will guide you through presenting your **previous employment**.

To gain the most from the book, you should read through this section, move on to the section(s) that are relevant to you, and finish with the final section.

General Introduction

The purpose of the employment section of your CV is to show the skills you have gained through experience. If you are adopting a **chronological format**, it should show a natural career progression.

Research

Before you begin to write, you will need to do a little research into the job. You should have the advertisement, and possibly a job description to help you. You can gain several clues from these.

The advertisement will make it clear that the company is looking for certain knowledge, skills and personal attributes.

Your **knowledge** is literally what you know. It may be academic knowledge (qualifications, degree, etc.), business knowledge (e.g., accounts or legal knowledge), or market/product knowledge (e.g., a computer programme or double-glazing sales).

Your **skills** are broadly the application of that knowledge (e.g., typing, handling customer complaints, telesales).

Attributes are your personal qualities (sense of humour, discretion, etc.).

You should note the clues within the advertisement that will tell you what the company is looking for in each of these, and then make sure your CV shows your relevant experience.

For example, if you are applying for work as an aerobics instructor, you will need to demonstrate some or all of the following knowledge, skills and attributes.

Knowledge: physiology, first-aid, safety issues, choreography.

Skills: choreography, leadership, motivation, dealing with people.

Attributes: friendly, approachable, lively, enthusiastic.

Note that choreography appears twice. Although you may assume that knowledge of how to choreograph an exercise routine implies the ability to actually put one together, any instructor will tell you that there are those who can and those who can't! You would therefore need to demonstrate that you know the technicalities and that you can put together a motivational routine.

Exercise: finding the clues

Take a look at the advertisements below and identify the knowledge, skills and attributes that the company require and any that would be preferable. (The answers are at the end of the section.)

GARAGE MANAGER

The 35 cars used by our sales staff and managers are chosen and bought by the users and funded by us. Staff can choose to buy new or second-hand vehicles subject to a budgetary limit and approval by their line manager. We also run a fleet of 20 light vans.

We are looking to recruit a garage manager to handle the booking of car and van servicing, etc., the administration of the fleet, insurance, etc. The job will also involve advising on suitability of purchase of cars and parts and the handling of routine maintenance between services.

The applicant will deal with staff at all levels and so will combine excellent communication skills, a professional presentation, and all-round mechanical ability.

You should have completed a recognized motor trade apprenticeship and have a combination of mechanical and administrative experience. This may be your first managerial position, but your work to date will make it a natural next step.

Knowledge: ____

____

Skills: ______________________________

____

____

Attributes: ______________________________

____

____

STORE MANAGER

You will be responsible for the hands-on running of one of our 14 successful music shops, specializing in up-to-the-minute music for a market of teenagers and young adults.

You will have proved yourself in a similar market and be committed to excellence in customer service, able to achieve financial targets and to be proactive in increasing the turnover of your store. You will already have led a team and used a computerized system for stock control. Your ability to merchandise your store and relate to your market will take you to the top with us.

You will work flexihours and weekends, and will need to spend approximately one day a month at our headquarters in London.

Knowledge: ____________________

____

____

Skills: ____________________

____

____

Attributes: ____________________

____

____

Once you have identified the knowledge, skills and attributes required for a job, you can then make sure that your CV demonstrates these qualifications, experience, and skills.

Of course, this should not be done specifically or in an obvious manner within your CV. It must remain factual, but you should emphasize the most relevant parts in your covering letter. (Example covering letters for the two exercises above are shown in Chapter 9 on covering letters.)

What to include

Unless you are just leaving school or college, the employment history is the most important part of your CV, and it is worth planning it carefully. To help you do this, follow the structured approach below.

1 Take a sheet of paper (or two!) and mark it into boxes or sections, one for each job you have had. If you have had many jobs, have one section for your earliest jobs combined.

2 Take the advertisement for the job you want, or take an example or two of similar jobs and identify the knowledge, skills and attributes that you need (see the exercise at the end of this section). For each item of knowledge, each skill and each attribute, note in your boxes where it is demonstrated. Do not worry if there are some duplications. If there are gaps, you could consider anything you do or have done in your spare time where you demonstrate the particular item.

3 When you have done this, go back over each job you have had and note any other specific experience you gained in each.

4 Double-check that you have not put in irrelevant or unimportant information which will take up valuable space and cloud the more important facts.

5 Select which examples you will include – you should avoid giving the same skill in every job outline.

6 Finally, take your notes on each job in turn and start to write them up as they will appear on your CV. Write and rewrite, reading them aloud, until they are concise and easy to read.

Precis the points rather than cutting out verbs or it will come over as hard and impersonal, not to mention difficult to read.

Remember, you should show the jobs you have had in reverse order, starting with the most recent or current one. This is the one which will have the most detail, and the amount written about each will usually decrease with each job. See 'Previous Employment' for further information.

Now turn to the section listed below that is relevant to you, and then finish with the final section to write up your previous jobs.

- *If you are employed*, turn to the following section and complete the box for your current job.
- *If you are planning a change in career, unemployed or returning after a career break*, turn to the relevant section and complete the boxes for your most recent job and your period away from work.
- *If you are a school or college leaver*, turn to the following section and complete the box for any vacation break or gap period.
- *Finally*, complete your employment *history* in the final section.

Sample answers

Below are some possible answers to the knowledge, skills, and attributes exercise.

Garage manager

Knowledge: mechanical; apprentice training; different vehicles specifications; insurance, etc.

Skills: motor maintenance; administrative; communication.

Attributes: smart appearance; friendly; sense of humour; careful.

Store manager

Knowledge: merchandising, computerized stock control, financial/accounting.

Skills: communication; dealing with buying public; supervisory.

Attributes: flexible; enthusiastic; energetic; suitable appearance.

Note that there is often a crossover between knowledge and skills, and that demonstrating the skill will often imply the knowledge. For example, a secretarial job that involves word-processing would not be possible without knowledge of the word processing program. It is enough, therefore, to mention that you are competent with the program. If you have a specific qualification, you should include it under 'Qualifications'.

Currently employed – want to move

The description you give of your current employment is probably the most important part of your CV. You have just a few lines to convince a prospective employer that your current experience makes you ideal for the post and that you will be able to slot into the existing team.

There is a fine line to be drawn between over- and underselling yourself. If you overdo it, you may make the reader ask, 'Why hasn't this person been promoted?' There may be perfectly genuine reasons, but there is no point in sowing the seeds of doubt. At the other end of the scale, of course, you must not undersell yourself. You are your own ambassador, and you must show your current job to be the perfect stepping-stone to the position you are applying for.

Relevant information

Think carefully about the skills and experience that the advertisement or job description outlines. Then, note at least one way in which you can demonstrate that you possess each one. If there are areas where you do not have current experience, think back over previous jobs, even sports or hobbies, and show these.

You should not, of course, show these in an obvious way in your CV. Make sure that every point is covered there and then draw attention to the most important ones in your covering letter.

Use logical groupings

Having assessed your experience in the light of the employer's requirements, you should group the information together logically in the outline of your job – often not the order of the advertisement!

There are four broad areas to consider:

- 'technical' abilities;
- supervisory/management skills;
- dealings with customers or clients;
- financial or budgetary responsibilities.

There is no obvious order for these – that will depend on the job you are applying for. For example, if you are applying for a job as a salesperson, your dealings with customers will be the most important aspect, and thus the first one outlined. If, however, you are applying for the post of manager in charge of the sales team, it may well be that your management skills will be of primary importance, followed by budgetary responsibilities.

The need to keep your CV short enough to be readable means that you will need to restrict yourself to a couple of sentences for the most important aspect of your experience, and one each for the less important areas. Remember, though, it is the importance of the job you are applying for that matters, not in relation to your current post.

You should not draw attention to any areas where you feel you are not well experienced in your CV or letter. However, it is a good idea to be prepared for questions at the interview!

Keep the outline of your current job to eight to ten lines – about four sentences – and think all the time of how it is going to look to the person who has written the advertisement – put yourself in their chair! For example:

1992-present **Public Relations Executive**
Amberway Business Park

- Established and maintained marketing campaign resulting in 85% occupancy at opening of Park.
- Generating ideas for and organized local events and on-site promotions.
- Managed major exhibitions on- and off-site.
- Liaison with press.
- Direct telephone research and promotions for Park.
- Co-ordination of administration for PR department (staff of two).

1992 to date **Budget Officer**, Montmarche International
I am responsible for the administration of budgets, department income and expenditure and job costing. I liaise with internal departments, other companies in the group and suppliers and have a particular interest in producing budgetary information in a user-friendly format. I prepare various management reports on variance, trend analysis and cost monitoring and help managers construct departmental budgets.

Designer, Abraham & Co **1989 onwards**
As one of three interior designers, I work mainly on large country houses and period, character homes, together with some commercial premises. I consult with clients in our offices, their homes/businesses, over the telephone, and through letters, reports and plans, and am responsible for liaising with suppliers and outworkers for my projects. I take control of each project from the initial meeting, through completing the work on time and to budget, and oversee the eventual installation and fitting. I also estimate for work, invoice my clients, and have project management and forward-planning responsibility.

1985– Branch Librarian

Personnel Management:	responsible for three staff.
Stock:	responsible for selection of books, videos and cassettes, revision of stock, and special orders.
Customers:	involvement with customers including dealing with enquiries, handling complaints, problem-solving and assisting with project work of students.
Administration:	banking and cash management, routine paperwork, shelving, catalogue updates and correspondence.

Write a successful CV – present employment

(dates) ____________ (position) ____________________________

(company/location) ____________________________

____

____

____

____

____

____

____

____

____

____

____

____

Checklist

Within your description of your present employment, have you:

- ☐ Grouped your skills and experience together logically?
- ☐ Put items in order of importance for the job you are applying for?
- ☐ 'Sold' yourself, phrasing information positively?

If you want a change

The biggest problem with a career change, from the point of view of a CV, is making your skills and experience to date seem relevant to an employer in a different field.

Add to this the problems caused by the entirely different cultures of various jobs, and you may find it very difficult to sell yourself in a field where your knowledge is limited.

An area where this is perhaps most pronounced is in the Services, where someone may have had a high level of responsibility, led people in difficult and dangerous situations, and have enormous technical skill, but have little perception of the interests of a recruitment manager.

Similarly, where people are changing between the public and private sectors, there can be barriers which need to be broken down. Using the right jargon and terminology will help this, as will placing the right emphasis on skills and experience.

If you have changed, or are changing, direction, your early work may not be particularly relevant now. In order to keep the emphasis away from where you have been and on what is relevant to the future, you might consider running the earliest posts together, particularly if they are similar and some time ago:

1968–1979 **SHIFT SUPERVISOR**
Pemberton Workwear, Glasgow

Daisy Knitwear, Glasgow
Having joined Pemberton Workwear company at 16 as a trainee machinist, I was promoted to senior machinist and later supervisor, responsible for the efficient working and quality of a team of 18 machinists.
In 1973 I joined Daisy Knitwear as supervisor, overseeing the work of two teams, and was promoted to senior supervisor, which included staffing the shifts, quality control and implementing cost-cutting measures.

A functional CV?

You may prefer to use a functional CV if you are changing direction because it will draw the emphasis away from a break in your career path and perhaps lack of experience in your new field. This will mean that you can give the information you want in the order that is relevant to the new employer. Because skills and experience are not related to specific jobs, you do not need to show where you gained them – it could have been some time ago or in a social situation. Use the exercise overleaf.

Write a successful CV – change of direction

For a chronological CV

Use the box below to outline your present employment with a view to your planned career move; in other words, the aspects that are important to the future.

(dates) ______ (position) ______________________

(company/location) ______________________

____

____

____

____

____

____

____

____

Exercise: Changing direction

To help you project yourself in a different field, work throug the stages below:

1 List your knowledge, skills and attributes below, citin evidence from your experience to date:

Knowledge

Skills

Attributes

2 Now turn to the advertisement, or an example advertisemen and again identify the knowledge, skills and attributes – this tim the ones specified by the employer.

Knowledge

Skills

____

____

____

____

Attributes

____

____

____

____

3 Note where the items match – these are points you should be emphasizing.

Note where there is a shortfall:

- If the employer is asking for skills you have not considered, go back over your work and social experience and try to find examples.
- If you have knowledge, skills, and attributes that are not relevant to the job, leave them out. No matter how impressive they are in their own right, if they do not actively sell you, omit them.

4 Finally, go through the notes you have made and cross out jargon – terminology that is specific to your previous work and experience. For example, an army officer may use the term 'commanded', whereas normal business usage would be 'led', or 'was responsible for . . .'. It may be helpful to ask someone in your chosen field to pick out words that are obviously out of place and perhaps suggest alternatives.

Note terms and expressions that are used in the advertisement and job descriptions and use these, where relevant, in your CV.

Write a successful CV – change of direction
For a functional CV

Depending on whether or not you are currently applying for a specific job, either:

1 identify the main areas the employer has given in the advertisement and use these as your headings, or,
2 consider the type of job you will be applying for and note the skills and experience you have gained under relevant headings. This can be amended when you apply for a specific job.

Note: In either case, the items identified here will be combined with skills and experience gained from past employment and leisure pursuits on your CV.

(heading) ______________________

- ______________________
- ______________________
- ______________________
- ______________________

(heading) ______________________

- ______________________
- ______________________
- ______________________
- ______________________

(heading) ____________________

- ____________________
- ____________________
- ____________________

Checklist

Have you:

- ☐ Identified the knowledge, skills, and attributes necessary for your new career?
- ☐ Emphasized your expertise in these areas, not in ones related to your previous jobs?
- ☐ (If functional) combined the skills and experience gained from all jobs and leisure, outlined in various sections of this book?

If You are Unemployed

It is an unhappy fact, but true, that it is easier to get a job if you already have one. When you are unemployed, the biggest problem is showing that you are still employable and have a positive attitude.

If you have been made redundant, try to show that you understand the company's point of view. There is no harm in admitting your disappointment, shock, or whatever, but if you can show that you are not bitter you will present a far more employable proposition. There is no need to make a big issue of this; it can be brought into your covering letter with statements like, 'My redundancy in 1993 was as a result of the lay off of 30% of the workforce across the board due to the financial difficulties the company was facing' – a simple statement of fact that makes it clear that the redundancy was not personal.

If the company ceased trading, make sure that your CV does not imply that you had any part in its downfall (not so easy if you were senior in the accounts or sales departments!).

If possible, show that you have used your time positively, studying a new subject, voluntary work and/or developing your skills. Be careful not to sound as though you have done *anything* to fill your time. You should present your activities in such a way that they clearly lead you to the post for which you are applying.

Leave out the things that have no relevance to your application, although do consider each to see if, viewed from a different angle, they say something positive and relevant about you.

Phrase your activities as though they were a job – business-like and professional. Avoid the trap of writing in a conversational style about a period of unemployment, in contrast to a business style for the rest of your CV.

If you have gained any specific qualifications, make sure that they are listed under 'Qualifications', although you would mention that you took the course in this section.

1993– Without employment
I have concentrated on seeking employment, and have attended local courses to develop and add to my existing skills. I have studied for and passed the examination for the Association of Accounting Technicians, and have studied French to conversational level. I have also been acting as treasurer to a local charity, streamlining their accounting system and teaching the paid manager the basics of bookkeeping. This role will finish when I return to full-time employment.

(Note the positive 'when I return . . .', not, 'if I return . . .'.

You should summarize your activities in this section, and can expand on how they support your suitability for the post you are applying for in the covering letter.

If you are not comfortable with the word 'unemployed', you can opt for one of the gentler alternatives, such as 'without employment'. Make sure that you do not take this to extremes, e.g., 'between employment'.

Unless you have enjoyed some success, avoid describing a period of unemployment as 'freelance consultancy'. It is an over-used euphemism, and tends to look negative because if you had been successful, you would have been unlikely to return to employment. It is more positive to list any freelance work as a subheading or subsection of 'without employment'.

While the 'without employment' section will be the first shown in your employment history, your last job will probably be the most detailed because it is likely to best demonstrate your relevant skills and experience.

A functional CV

A functional CV will draw attention away from current or previous periods of employment because the emphasis is on the skills and experience you have, rather than when or the way in which you gained them.

Always keep the requirements of the job you are applying for at the front of you. Decide on the headings you will use (from clues in the advertisement) and then choose key points to demonstrate your suitability in these areas. It does not matter whether these come from previous employment or things you have done during periods of unemployment, but you should not show which.

Example: functional CV

Bob, whose CV yielded the extract given earlier in this section, left school with 'O'-levels in mathematics and accounting. Based on this he had got a job as junior in the accounts department of a manufacturing company. After three promotions, he was debt-recovery manager before being made redundant in early 1993. He is now applying for the job of assistant manager, accounts, a more general job in a much smaller company, but one whose client base is largely in Europe. His functional CV might look like this:

ROBERT NICHOLAS

96 Elm Tree Gardens
Longstock
Devon
Tel: (0987) 654321

PROFESSIONAL EXPERIENCE

- Five years' general accounting experience.
- Sole responsibility for debt recovery (reduced outstanding debt to less than 5%).
- Member of the Association of Accounting Technicians.
- Experience of streamlining an outdated accounting system.

LANGUAGES

- Fluent French.
- Written and conversational German.

INTERPERSONAL SKILLS

- Able to communicate effectively with clients at all levels.
- Persuasive but polite and friendly in approach.
- Enjoy working as part of a team.

Write a successful CV – without employment
For a chronological CV

(dates) ______ (heading) ______

For a functional CV

Depending on whether or not you are currently applying for a specific job, either:

1 identify what the employer is looking for and note any skills or experience that you have gained from your period of unemployment that will support your application, or,
2 consider the type of job you will be applying for and note the skills and experience you have gained under relevant headings. This can be amended when you apply for a specific job.

Note: In either case, the items identified here will be combined with the skills and experience gained from past employment and leisure pursuits on your CV.

(heading) ____________________

- ____________________
- ____________________
- ____________________
- ____________________

(heading) ____________________

- ____________________
- ____________________
- ____________________
- ____________________

(heading)
____

- ______________________________
- ______________________________
- ______________________________

Checklist

Have you:

- ☐ Ensured that you have used positive words and do not sound bitter?
- ☐ Presented your time away from work as though it has been preparation for just this job?
- ☐ (If functional) combined the skills and experience gained from all jobs and leisure, outlined in various sections of this book?

Returning to work after a break

If you are returning to work because, for example, your children are now at school, it can be difficult to convince an employer that you are committed to a return to work and that you are specifically interested in the particular job (as opposed to any job to get you out of the house or bring in some money).

If you are returning to the type of work you did before the break, you should outline your previous employment, as shown at the end of this section. Obviously, your time spent at home will be the first part, as the most recent, but it should have equal space, or second billing, to your last employment. Note anything you have done which will demonstrate your strengths to a potential employer – voluntary work, running or helping with toddler groups, hearing readers at primary school – can all be shown to be of benefit. These should be outlined in the employment section, and the benefits they bring to a prospective employer can be dealt with in the covering letter.

1987–1993 **Career break**
While at home with two children, I served as treasurer for the under-fives group, and worked on the committee for the town carnival.

If you have updated your skills, this can be mentioned under 'Career Break' with any qualifications you gained as a result shown in 'Qualifications':

1985–1992 **Career break**
During this period at home with my family, I registered as a childminder and looked after up to three children during the day. I was elected to the PTA of my son's school, with responsibility for fundraising. During 1993 I attended the City College to update my skills and study wordprocessing (see Qualifications).

If you are hoping to return to a completely different career, it is essential to try to slant your CV so that the progression to your chosen path is obvious. If, for example, you previously worked as a secretary but now want to change direction to your long-term love, the theatre, you should give emphasis to the qualifications suitable for a career in the theatre. Similarly, the brief summaries of your previous work should stress aspects that will relate to the work you want to do, rather than what was important at the time.

Translating your experience

If you have been at home in the role of carer for a period of time, it can be difficult to translate your experience into business skills, both in terms of recognizing the value of your skills, and then phrasing them in business terminology.

You should first think of what you have been doing, and then consider the benefits this experience will bring to a business. Finally, look at it from the employer's point of view and choose suitable terms. Below are some examples:

Experience	**Business skill**
Served on committee for fundraising event.	'Served on committee for centenary celebrations, working with local businessmen and women to raise a total of £1000.'
Helped at senior citizens' day centre.	'Worked at local day centre for senior citizens: special interest in collating information for regular newsletter and tape.'
Member of the PTA.	'Was a member of school PTA for three years, contributed to decisions about the day-to-day management of the school.'
Helped at playgroup.	'Joined a team of four helpers at local playgroup, assisting the leader three days a week.'

Any treasury experience, e.g., playgroup or other committee.	'Appointed treasurer of local playgroup, with responsibility for management of funds, invoicing, and cash book.'

A functional CV

A functional CV will often benefit the returner because it draws attention away from the career break and emphasizes the relevant skills and experience you have, rather than when, or the way in which, you gained them.

Using the knowledge, skills and attributes approach outlined earlier, identify what the employer is looking for in terms of broad headings, and then decide how you can demonstrate that you satisfy each criterion.

Example: functional CV

Sally wants to return to work now her children are in full-time school. Previously a PA, she is applying for the post of secretary in a local construction firm. She is aware of the disadvantages of a career break, and wants to build up her skills and confidence. She also knows she must avoid stressing how senior a post she held before in case she gives the impression that she will bore easily of her new job and leave. The advertisement asked for 'good secretarial skills, the ability to deal with customers over the telephone, ability to work on own initiative under pressure, and sense of humour'. Her CV might look like this:

Curriculum Vitae

Sally Marchant
Hillview, Vicarage Road, Amblestone, Herts.
(0111 456321)

Secretarial skills

- Fast and accurate typist.
- Experienced wordprocessor operator (Wordperfect and Wordstar).
- Shorthand at 100wpm.
- Audio-typing.

Dealings with customers and colleagues

- Long experience of dealing with customers over the telephone.
- Used to working on own initiative over periods of several days.
- Experience of working within the construction industry.
- Able to deal with customers and colleagues at all levels.

Personal attributes

- Cheerful and enthusiastic.
- Flexible in approach with a positive attitude.
- Enjoys work and committed to high standards.

Exercise: consider your experience

Note down the things that you have done while at home (even if they seem very ordinary) in the left-hand column, and turn the most relevant of them into 'business-speak' in the right-hand column:

Things you have done	**'Business-speak'**

Write a successful CV – career break

For a chronological CV

(date) ______	Career Break ______
	______
	______
	______
	______
	______
	______

For a functional CV

Depending on whether or not you are currently applying for a specific job, either:

1 identify what the employer is looking for and note any skills or experience that you have gained from your career break that will support your application, or,

2 consider the type of job you will be applying for and note the skills and experience you have gained under relevant headings. This can be amended when you apply for a specific job.

Note: In either case, the items identified here will be combined with skills and experience gained from past employment on your CV.

A functional CV

(heading) ______________________________

- ______________________________
- ______________________________
- ______________________________

(heading) ______________________________

- ______________________________
- ______________________________
- ______________________________

(heading) ______________________________

- ______________________________
- ______________________________
- ______________________________

Checklist

Have you:

- [ ] Included things you have done while at home, and shown them in a positive light?
- [ ] Used business terms, even when describing non-business activities?
- [ ] (If using a functional CV), mixed skills and experience gained at home with that gained in previous work?

School, college, or university leaver

Do not feel that you have to pad out your CV for the sake of it. It is far preferable to have one page of relevant information than two giving every conceivable detail, regardless of its worth to potential employers.

Since your academic achievements are likely to be of more interest than your work experience, it is worthwhile putting in grades. If you have a diploma or degree, you should leave out your GCSE grades, but include the others. Arrange your qualifications with the most advanced first, and end with your GCSEs.

Within each group, arrange the subjects in the order of most relevance to the jobs you are applying for. A grade 'A' in music may be your highest achievement, but a 'B' in a science will be of most interest if you want a technical job.

If you give any grades within a section, give all of them, otherwise you will only make an employer suspicious.

1993 HND Business Studies

1991 GCE 'A' Levels: Economics (B), English (B), Biology (A)

1989 GCE 'O' Levels: English language, English literature, Mathematics, French, Biology and Food and Nutrition

Vacation work

If you have worked during your holidays, you should mention this because it shows that you are motivated and that you have some experience. Concentrate on the jobs you have done that are relevant to the type of work you are seeking, if only in terms of the skills demonstrated. If none of them are relevant, try to show a broad spread of skills demonstrated, e.g., the ability to deal with members of the public, to handle basic bookkeeping, to use a specified system.

Long-term jobs

If you have had long-term vacation jobs (either a full vacation, or where you have returned to the same job in each vacation over a period), list them as you would full-time employment, but starting with the one which shows you in the best light, rather than the most recent first as you would with full-time employment. You can then combine any lower-key ones together at the end.

Short-term/temporary jobs

If you have done a variety of short-term temporary jobs, they can be shown as below:

Summer 1993	**Temporary work** A varicty of short-term assignments, the major ones being: 1 **Waitressing**, working as part of a team at private and public functions, helping customers at the buffet table, clearing tables, serving drinks, etc. 2 **Despatch assistant**, acting as runner for a team of despatch staff, assisting in the packing and checking process, preparing parcels for despatch.

The description above highlights the applicant's experience of working in a team, dealing with the public, and undertaking tasks that need accuracy and care. The two job areas are different and will need different skills. Assuming that good references would be given, they are of positive benefit to someone applying for a job requiring any of these skills.

An alternative way of showing what you have done in a positive way and of showing you understand the needs of business is to briefly outline a vacation job or project and then demonstrate what you have gained from it.

If you have been part of a voluntary group working to clear an overgrown canal, you could use this to demonstrate the following:

'Whilst with the South Dorset Canal Restoration Project I . . .'

Problem-solving skills	'. . . worked in small group to decide best strategy for overcoming day-to-day problems faced by the team.'
Ability to work within team	'. . . was part of a team from assorted professional backgrounds, united by the desire to open up this stretch of the canal.'
Leadership	'. . . led groups of occasional volunteers, students and helpers with learning difficulties, and working on specific tasks within the project.'
Presentation skills	'. . . spoke to various local groups and schools about the project.'

Think about your leisure time and consider what your activities say about you to an employer. Look for examples of leadership, initiative, dealing with finance (e.g., treasurer of a club), working as part of a team. Try to show a balance, and do not give the impression that your sport or hobbies are more important to you than anything else. To be captain of the under-16s is certainly worthy, but you do not want to give the impression that you will be totally preoccupied with life on the field or may suffer from injuries.

Remember that from the point of view of the employer, you are untested in the 'real' world. Apart from your academic qualifications, try to show staying power, commitment to whatever you are doing, and a willingness to mix and fit in.

Write a successful CV – vacation work

Decide how you can best show your work experience and complete the box below.

____
____
____
____
____
____
____
____

Checklist

Have you:

- ☐ Listed your qualifications before your work experience?
- ☐ Used business English to describe your work experience?
- ☐ Outlined the jobs that show you in the best light?

Previous employment

If you have chosen to use a chronological CV, you will need to list the jobs you have held throughout your working life.

However, there is limited space, and if your working history is long, you will not be able to list every job and in any case, the early ones are unlikely to be relevant.

You should only show three or, at most, four jobs in addition to your current or most recent one. They should be shown in reverse order (continuing with the strategy of most recent first), with the choice of what to include governed by the job you are applying for (see the first part of section on employment history to help you decide what is relevant). The amount of information given for each job will reduce as you work backwards, so that your first or earliest post will probably have only two or three lines.

Bear in mind that you should try to show a logical career progression both in job titles and in the work you did in each post.

Headings

The information of most interest to a potential employer is the position you held, not the company name, therefore each position should be headed with the position before the company and location:

1986–1991 OFFICE MANAGER
Ellsmore & Co., Bristol (Architects)

This layout means that by scanning the positions you have held, the reader can get a feel for your career path.

Combining early posts

If you are to keep your CV to two sheets of paper, you are unlikely to have space for more than three or four previous positions. If you have been employed for many years and have held several posts, you should consider combining the early two or three, particularly if you have progressed a long way since then.

If you held a few similar posts, these can be shown as:

1972–1977	**ACCOUNTS CLERK**
1972–1974	**Ashburton Mouldings,** Manchester
1974–1975	**Applied Components,** Manchester
1975–1977	**Maplow Engineering,** Manchester
	These posts involved computerized accounting, debt recovery, cash-book and ledger entry.

Alternatively, if the posts were different, you could show them as:

1968–1975	Variety of short-term posts, including sales assistant, bookkeeping and clerical work.

It is unlikely that any of these posts will demonstrate skills which you want to emphasize now. However, if any of them are relevant, it is best to emphasize them by laying it out as in the first of the two examples above, or not to bunch them together at all.

When you get on to the posts you have held which have a direct relevance to the one you are applying for, you should give more detail. Do not repeat the same facts for each job unless you have to (e.g., secretarial jobs almost always include typing and shorthand or audio). If the same responsibilities keep coming up, try to find a suitable coverall (e.g., usual secretarial duties), and then emphasize what is different about each post.

Do not go into long descriptions of every aspect of each job. It is important that the employer can see how your career has progressed, and so each description should give the tasks you took on in addition to your previous work. It will usually be obvious which more menial tasks have dropped off the bottom of your work.

1986–1991 **OFFICE MANAGER**
Ellsmore & Co., Bristol (Architects)
My responsibilities included the management of every aspect of the administrative support for the firm, supervision of six clerical staff and management of all office systems, including the installation of a network computer system.

Promotions

If you have been employed by one company for some time and have held several different posts, these should usually be presented as separate jobs. By leaving the headings as below, it is clear that you have stayed with the same company:

1986–1991 **OFFICE MANAGER**
Ellsmore & Co., Bristol (Architects)
My responsibilities included the management of every aspect of the administrative support for the firm, supervision of six clerical staff and management of all office systems, including the installation of a network computer system.

1984–1986 **Administrator/PA**
I was responsible for the main administrative systems and provided secretarial support to the senior partner.

1982–1984 **Secretary**
I worked directly for two managers and handled the typing for their technical staff.

1980–1982 **Receptionist/shorthand typist**
I was responsible for operating the switchboard and greeting all visitors. I also handled routine typing.

Alternatively, the applicant might wish to gloss over the secretarial role, having moved to a managerial position and thus would break the 'most-recent-first' rule within the three early posts as below:

EMPLOYMENT HISTORY

1986–1991	**OFFICE MANAGER** **Ellsmore & Co.,** Bristol (Architects) My responsibilities included the management of every aspect of the administrative support for the firm, supervision of six clerical staff and management of all office systems, including the installation of a network computer system.
1980–1986	**Ellsmore & Winterton, Bristol** After joining the firm as a **receptionist**/shorthand typist, I was promoted to **secretary** in 1982. I worked for a team of managers and technical staff and took responsibility for all secretarial duties, prioritizing work and dealing with client enquiries. In 1984 I was promoted to **personal assistant** to work solely for the senior partner and also took on responsibility for the updating of the office systems, introduction of computers, etc.

Temporary work

If your experience includes a period temping, do not show every assignment. Instead, show the dates as above, the name and location of the agency or just 'temporary work'. If any of your temp jobs are particularly relevant for the post you are applying for, you can mention the fact in your covering letter. Show a general outline of what the work involved, including only the specific items that are relevant:

1989–1991	**Temporary Work, Birmingham** A variety of temporary jobs covering all aspects of office work in professional and commercial companies. Included taking minutes at meetings, customer service support, and data processing.

Reason for leaving

Do not give a reason for leaving in your CV. It is almost impossible to give a reason that sounds positive, and even career advancement can make it sound as though you changed jobs regularly to gain a step up the ladder. Remember that employers want people who will stay for a reasonable period of time and show loyalty to their employer. Too much ambition may not make you look attractive.

Write a successful CV – employment history

For a chronological CV

In the boxes below, outline your previous employment history, *excluding* your most recent job.

(date) ____________ (position) ____________________________

(company/location) ____________________________

(responsibilities) ____________________________

____

____

____

(date) ____________ (position) ____________________________

(company/location) ____________________________

(responsibilities) ____________________________

____

____

____

(date) ____________ (position) ____________

(company/location) ____________

(responsibilities) ____________

(date) ____________ (position) ____________

(company/location) ____________

(responsibilities) ____________

A functional CV

Depending on whether or not you are currently applying for a specific job, either:

1 Identify what the employer is looking for and note any skills or experience that you have gained from your previous jobs break that will support your application, or,
2 consider the type of job you will be applying for and note the skills and experience you have gained under relevant headings. This can be amended when you apply for a specific job.

Note: In either case, the items identified here will be combined with skills and experience gained from your current employment, time away from work, etc. on your CV.

(heading) ______________________________

• ______________________________

• ______________________________

• ______________________________

(heading) ______________________________

• ______________________________

• ______________________________

• ______________________________

(heading) ________________________

- ________________________
- ________________________
- ________________________

Checklist

Have you:

- [ ] Worked backwards through your previous jobs?
- [ ] Shown a logical career progression in job titles and job content?
- [ ] Given less detail for earlier jobs?
- [ ] (If using a functional CV), mixed skills and experience from past employment with current information?

4

Education and qualifications

Many people show education and qualifications as one section, with the two mixed together; for example, using the school or college as a heading, and listing the qualifications gained under each:

EDUCATION & QUALIFICATIONS

1992–1994 **The Tertiary College, Swinburn**
GCE 'A' Levels: English (B), Human Biology (B), and French (C)

1986–1992 **King Davids School, Swinburn**
GCSE: English Language, Mathematics, Biology, Physics, Art, French and German

The problem with this style is that it puts the emphasis on your school or college rather than your achievements. The employer is far more interested in the qualifications you have gained than in the place where you gained them. With this in mind, it is preferable to show education and qualifications separately with qualifications first:

QUALIFICATIONS

1994 GCE 'A' Levels: English (B), Human Biology (B), and French (C)

1992 GCSE: English Language, Mathematics, Biology, Physics, Art, French and German

EDUCATION

1992–1994 The Tertiary College, Swinburn
1986–1992 King Davids School, Swinburn

Note that in both the above examples, the most recent education and the highest qualifications come first. This is because an employer will read down from the start of the section and can merely pass on to the next section when they feel they have read enough. If the most important information is at the bottom of the section, it is possible they will pass on before they read it.

Education

When giving the schools and colleges you have attended, you need only give the name and town, not the full address. If you have attended two secondary schools, you should give both, but if you have been at more, it is best to mention this by giving the overall dates and saying 'various schools'. In this case give the one or two at which you sat examinations:

EDUCATION

1984–1986 St Edmunds Comprehensive, Elverton
1980–1984 Various schools

Qualifications

Unless you are just leaving school or college, it is not necessary to give your grades. However, if you want to, you must give all the grades within a section, not just the good ones. In other words, if you show your grades for a couple of 'O' levels, you must show them for all 'O' levels.

However, if you have 'A' levels and/or higher qualifications, you do not need to show your 'O' level grades at all. In summary, if you are going to show any grades, show them for your highest set of academic qualifications.

Although most people do give the dates of examinations, there is no particular need. An alternative layout which saves spacc and improves the visual impact is to lay qualifications as below:

QUALIFICATIONS

Diploma Chartered Institute of Marketing

Degree BA (Hons) History of Art

A-levels History of Art, English, Geography

O-levels English Literature, English Language, Mathematics, History, Geography, Biology, French

If you wished, you could put the dates in brackets at the end of each group.

Qualifications

A qualification is a subject in which you have passed an examination. You can show the year in which you took the qualification, and should give its title and where relevant, any grade you achieved. Try to avoid initials or shortened versions of the title; the recruiter may not recognize it for what it is.

Group your qualifications together logically with the most important first, based on its relevance to the job(s) you are applying for. Your qualifications will usually then go in order of descending importance.

If, however, you have changed or are changing, careers, you should start with the one which is most relevant to the work you are seeking, even if this is a lower level than the qualifications in your previous field.

Where you have achieved improved qualifications, e.g., shorthand at 70, 80, and 90wpm, you should only show the fastest. Similarly, if you have Grades I and II typewriting, you should only show the Grade II.

One exception to the 'rules' of giving qualifications is with computer work, e.g., word processing. While a qualification in wordprocessing is certainly relevant, the programs you can use is of equal importance, particularly if you can use more than one or are proficient in the one requested in the advertisement. If this is the case, give the qualification, then the programs:

1991 Wordprocessing, RSA Grade 2
Experienced WordPerfect, Word, Decmate
Typewriting, RSA Grade 3
Audio typewriting, RSA Grade 2

Degrees

You should show a degree or post-graduate qualification by the title and the class. Mention any special subjects, research or papers only where relevant, and if you feel it would benefit you, expand upon this in your covering letter.

If you have an Open University degree, do not list all the subjects in which you gained credits, just the main courses.

Diplomas, etc.

The principle is much the same as for a degree. Make sure that you display the qualification in such a way that it will be understood by a non-specialist.

Where the examination does not have a specific name, but qualifies you for membership of an institute, it is best to put it as follows to show that you have passed the examination (rather than gained an exemption):

> Diploma of the Institute of Training & Development

If you are a member of the relevant institute, this can be shown under 'Other Information'.

If you have gained your diploma through an exemption, you should bite the bullet and say so, avoiding the implication that you are better qualified than is true. However, this need not be done in an apologetic way. Describe your means of gaining an exemption in a clear, concise sentence, naming any relevant papers presented, etc.

In theory, this should go under 'Other Information'. However, if an employer is going to be looking under 'Qualifications', it will need to be there if she is not to assume that you do not have membership of the particular institute. You have two options:

1 put the relevant initials after your name at the head of the CV and outline your exemption under 'Other Information', or,

2 outline your exemption under 'Qualifications' along the lines below:

1992 **Member of Institute of Training and Development**
Gained membership by an exemption on presentation of a paper outlining research, design, development and evaluation of training for secretarial staff in my industry combined with details of my current work and client comments.

'A' levels

Once you have been employed for a few years, grades cease to be relevant, particularly if you have a degree or diploma. You may, however, wish to show them if you are changing direction and your best 'A' level grades relate to your new career rather than your original one.

GCSE/'O' level

The system of grading has changed several times over the past thirty years, with the same grade being a pass or a fail at different times. If you show grades, make sure it is clear that you have passed those you give.

If you have gone on to take 'A' levels or a degree, the 'O' level grades you obtained are irrelevant and will merely clutter the page.

Other qualifications

If something like driving is essential for the job, you might wish to show the fact that you hold a licence, particularly in this case, if you have passed the advanced test. There is no specified place to put information like this, but it should sit with the more 'adult' qualifications, and therefore should be placed above 'A' levels.

Competent but not qualified

If a job specifically requires something like a language in which you are fluent but do not have a formal qualification, it should still be put in this section because this is where an employer will look.

Languages

French: fluent, business and conversation.
Italian: basic command.

This type of entry should *only* be used when the skill is specifically required. If overdone it will clutter the CV and detract from it.

Training courses

If the training courses are not specifically relevant to the job you are applying for, these are best listed under 'Other Information'. It is rare that any merit a place in 'Qualifications', but if you feel that one is vital to your ability to do the job you are applying for, it can be listed.

However, use a separate heading to show that you understand the difference between attending a short course and gaining a qualification. If you have attended many, only show the most important/relevant – beware of looking like a professional course attender.

To finish, two examples of applicants who take in the above points. They have used different layouts, to help you compare and decide which suits you best.

QUALIFICATIONS

1992	MBA, Cranfield School of Management
1983	B.Sc., Biology
1980	A-levels: Biology, Chemistry, English
1978	O-levels: Biology, Chemistry, English, Maths, French, Geography

EDUCATION

1980–1983	Brunel University
1973–1980	Milburn Hill School, Lincoln

QUALIFICATIONS

Degree: BA (Hons) English

Language: French, business & conversational

'A' levels: English Literature, Geography, Art

'O' levels: English, History, Geography, Art, RE, Biology

EDUCATION

London University (1986–1989)

King John's School, Watstone (1980–1985)

Note: in the above example, the applicant's knowledge of French could be explained under 'Other Information', perhaps travel during a gap year, etc.

Write a successful CV – qualifications

TECHNICAL/
PROFESSIONAL

(date) ______ (qualification) ______________________

____

____

(date) ______ (qualification) ______________________

____

____

(date) ______ (qualification) ______________________

____

____

(date) ______ (qualification) ______________________

____

____

(date) ______ (qualification) ______________________

____

ACADEMIC

(date) ________ (degree) ________________________

____

____

(date) ________ (diploma, etc.) ________________________

____

____

(date) ________ ('A'-levels) ________________________

____

____

____

(date) ________ (GCSE/O-levels) ________________________

____

____

____

____

Write a successful CV – education

(date) ______	(university) ______
(date) ______	(college) ______
(date) ______	(secondary school/s) ______
	______
	______
	______

Checklist

Have you:

- ☐ Shown only subjects where you have passed an examination or where you are highly competent in an area that is vital to the job?
- ☐ Shown the most important first in each area?
- ☐ Been consistent in showing your grades within each section?

5

Other information

This section should include any information which is of sufficient importance to be included in your CV, but does not naturally fall into any previous category. This is the place to give details of your date of birth, marital status, and so on – things that would take up too much space on the front page, and in any case are not sufficiently important to receive such prominence.

You do not need to include all of the following. There may also be information you wish to give which is not outlined below. The criterion to use in deciding what to include is 'will this information be a positive benefit to my CV?'

The most common facts found in 'Other Information' include the following.

Date of birth/age

Although you may not like to give your date of birth, not to do so tends to look suspicious. It is preferable to include it because an employer can work it out from your education and employment history if they want, and you have more to gain from making life easy for the reader. If you want to include your age, make sure you amend it with each birthday. When you proofread your CV, make sure you have not fallen into the trap of putting this year's date – many job applicants are only a few months old according to their CV!

Marital status

Although historically this is included on CVs, it is not usually relevant. However, most employers expect it, so you may want to include it – it is personal choice. Remember, though, that if you are female and say you are married, expect questions about your current or planned family!

Children

Opinion here is divided. If you mention young children, an employer may well look upon you less favourably, suspecting that you will take more time off. If you do not say, the assumption may well be either 'has children and not saying', or 'likely to have children soon'. If you opt for not mentioning your children, it is best to omit your marital status as well so as to be consistent in not giving personal information on your CV. You must be prepared for a surprised response from an interviewer and plan your answer if you are asked why you omitted to mention them.

Driving licence

It is not really necessary to say 'clean' unless this would be important to the job. If holding a licence is critical for the job, for example as a sales representative on the road, you should include it under 'Qualifications'.

Languages

Any formal language qualifications will have appeared under 'Qualifications'. However, if you are unqualified but have a conversational, working, or fluent command of a language this is the place to mention it. If a language is essential for the job you are applying for and you have a sufficient knowledge of that language but no formal qualification, you should put it under a separate heading within 'Qualifications' because this is where the employer will look.

Professional bodies

If you are a member of a professional body or institute and this is separate from your qualification, note it. This is particularly relevant where you have become a member on an exemption but want to make it clear you are a member. In this instance, it may be worth putting the initials after your name.

Health

It is not necessary to give the status of your health unless it is specifically relevant to the work you do (e.g., fitness instructor).

Disability

There are opposing views as to whether it is preferable to mention any disability at this stage, or leave the interviewer to find out face-to-face. If you decide you want to include it on a CV, make sure you give a brief non-clinical description of your disability and keep the emphasis on what you can do, rather than on what you can't. If you decide to leave it out, be prepared to answer questions at interview.

Referees

You should not give referees on a CV. If you wish to show you are happy for a prospective employer to take up references, put 'References available on request'. It is highly unlikely that anyone would want to take up references before an interview, and you will need to know who is going to contact whom, so that you can politely forewarn them. To give names and addresses on a CV is a waste of valuable space.

Current salary

It is not wise to put this on a CV. If it is too high you may be discounted because of the assumption that you will not work for less; if too low, you may be offered a lower salary with a new job because few employers will pay more than they have to. It is preferable to get to the stage of talking terms before committing yourself. Do, however, consider how you will answer the question, 'What salary are you looking for?' at interview.

Layout

The layout for 'Other Information' should match the other sections. It is best not to run the information together, narrative style, because important facts can get lost that way. Either use subheadings or bullet points as shown in the examples below.

OTHER INFORMATION

Date of Birth: 23 March 1966.
Driving Licence: full licence, clean, 10 years' experience.
Languages: French (conversational).
Referees: Available on request.

OTHER INFORMATION

- Date of birth: 28 January 1943. Age 51.
- Full driving licence.
- Member, Institute of Personnel Management.
- Status: married, two children.
- Referees available on request.

Write a successful CV – other information

____
____
____
____
____
____
____
____
____
____

Checklist

Have you:

- ☐ Checked your year of birth (make sure it is not the current year)?
- ☐ Only put in relevant information that is of positive benefit to your CV?

6
Hobbies and pastimes

The seemingly innocent question of what you do with your spare time can be a minefield. For example:

- if you say 'nothing' you may appear a dull couch potato;
- if you express a passion for a particular sport, you might alienate an employer with a particular bias or prejudice against it;
- hobbies like sailing can give the impression of long weekends (and late appearances on Mondays);
- a solitary pastime such as reading or embroidery might give the impression that you are unwilling to mix and are not good at being part of a team;

  and so on . . .

Of course, if you quote a sport or hobby and find that your enthusiasm is shared by the employer, you may find that it furthers your cause. However, at the time of writing your CV you will be most unlikely to know anything of his or her interests and so can only take a balanced approach and hope for the best.

Your aim should be to show a balance. Ideally, something that shows you can work well as part of a team, perhaps an example of leadership (team captain, for example) balanced by a more solitary pastime. You should try to avoid showing only solitary hobbies, giving the impression of difficulty in mixing, or only gregarious pastimes, which might give the impression of play being more important than work.

Do not be tempted to show too many outside work activities – the employer might wonder how you fit in time to work.

Hobbies and Pastimes

Cricket and tennis at social level. On a quieter note, I enjoy reading and fly-fishing.

If your hobbies do not appear balanced, but in fact are because of your involvement, you should show that all is not as it appears on the surface:

Hobbies and Pastimes

Reading, correspondence with penfriends, model-boat building (social secretary and race for team in county league).

Do not be tempted to 'justify' every hobby – save it for occasions when it matters and when it will have an impact. If you can show a balance of pastimes, there is no need to give an explanation.

Write a successful CV – hobbies

In the box below, list your hobbies as you wish them to appear on your CV. Remember to justify *only* those where you particularly wish to show there is more to your pastime than may be obvious.

Checklist

Have you:

- [ ] Shown a balanced group of pastimes?
- [ ] Noted or justified only in special cases?

7
Presentation and layout

You cannot overestimate the importance of the layout and visual presentation of your CV. This is not to say that it should be typeset. Although this is easy to have done these days, it looks impersonal and many employers are not comfortable reading something so regimented!

The CV should give the impression of reflecting someone who is extremely professional and highly competent. If you can send in a CV that is well laid out on good-quality paper and free of spelling and grammatical mistakes you will already be ahead of much of the competition. Lets look at the various aspects in more detail.

Initial impressions

The first impression is vital. If someone has to read tens, if not hundreds, of CVs, it is easy to put the untidy ones on the 'reject' pile, however unintentionally, and concentrate on those that look easy to read.

Your CV should be typed on A4 paper and be pristine, either very well photocopied or printed off specially. There should be no smudges, coffee stains or other marks, and it should be folded as few times as possible, ideally not at all. The sheets should be stapled together neatly.

If possible, use a better-quality paper than the normal copier bond – preferably the 100gsm that is used for quality letterheads. Although this may not be immediately noticeable to the eye, it gives an overall impression of quality and feels good in the hand of the employer. This is the CV equivalent of 'body language', which may not be obvious to the conscious mind, but sends a more powerful message than words. A good-quality paper and professional layout send a strong and positive message about you at little extra cost.

Spelling

Spelling mistakes say a number of things about you to a potential employer. For example, you are poorly educated, you are lazy, you are careless, and so on.

There is no excuse for spelling mistakes. Use a spell-checker if you have one, but remember that it will not show up mistakes such as 'not/now' or 'from/form'. Use a dictionary for any words that you are not completely sure of and find a friend who can spell to read your CV through for you.

Grammar and style

Read your CV out loud. If it does not read well, your grammar needs adjusting. Ask a friend to read it through.

Decide whether you want to use paragraphs of text or notes, and stick to the same throughout. Paragraphs are easier to read, but bullets save space and are more 'punchy'. If you decide on bullets, still keep to sentences to make your CV easy to read. Whichever you opt for, make sure you are consistent throughout all sections of your CV.

Think about where you break paragraphs. It is unlikely that any section of your CV will need more than one paragraph, but they are relevant for your covering letter. A new paragraph starts a new piece of information, not inserted because the existing paragraph is getting too long. If this is happening, precis the long paragraph; do not break it for the sake of it.

Typing

There are certain 'rules' for typing which are invaluable. Although you may not like being constricted by regulations, it is worth remembering that they are there for a purpose – to make the document easy on the eye and easy to read.

Some of the most basic (and most useful ones) are:

- keep to one typeface throughout, both for headings and text, although you can alter the size of headings if you wish;
- two spaces after a full stop and colon;
- one space after a comma and semicolon;
- two lines between paragraphs;
- the left margin wider than the right, usually by a quarter of an inch;

- the top margin wider than the bottom usually by a quarter or half-inch;
- consistency of style, e.g., headings of the same importance in the same style/size, dates in same format throughout, etc.

'White' space

The 'white' space is the part of the paper that is not covered with typing. Do not be tempted to type close to the edge of the paper and cram your paragraphs together in an effort to keep your CV to the limit of two pages. Precis the content instead! Ideally you should have:

Top/bottom margin:	three-quarters of an inch/half an inch, or one inch/three quarters of an inch (half an inch if you are going to have a page number at the bottom).
Left/right margin:	one-and-a-quarter inches/one inch, or one inch/three quarters of an inch.

'White' space also involves the space between paragraphs and sections. There should always be a blank line between paragraphs, and it looks clearer if you leave two blank lines between sections.

Layout

The key to good layout is consistency. Keep to the same margins, the same tab stops and the same layout for each section paragraph. The only exception to this is your name and address, etc. (assuming you keep to only the name, address and telephone number).

Examples

ELEANOR JACKSON
Orchard House, 21 Thames Road,
Broadbank, RG24 7MG
(0243) 123456

EMPLOYMENT HISTORY

Sales Manager **1991-present**
Aboco Paper plc, Reading, Berkshire
- Report to sales director.
- Contact with directors, heads of purchasing, etc.
- Responsible for team of 8 sales staff.
- Annual turnover of £7m.
- Member of management strategy team, with special responsibility for new trends.

Assistant Sales Manager **1986–1991**
Graphcon, Basildon, Essex
- Promoted from initial position of salesperson.
- Responsible for building up new customer base.
- Involved in provision of technical support to sales staff and customers.
- In charge of administration aspects of office.

QUALIFICATIONS

Diploma, Institute of Sales and Marketing (1991)

CURRICULUM VITAE

DANIEL FORSTONE

Address: 11 Heronsbrook
Halversone Leigh
Nr. York

Telephone: (0243) 123456

EMPLOYMENT HISTORY

1993– **Seeking Employment**
While actively looking for work, I have studied French and marketing at college. I have also led a team of volunteers working to clear an acre of derelict woodland. This has improved my skills of project management, leadership, and motivation, and the resulting 'wild play area' is a benefit to residents of our town.

1989–1993 **Office Manager**
Harcron & Davis, York
Responsible to the senior partner, I was in charge of all aspects of the office including accounts, purchasing, secretarial.

Checklist

Does your CV:

- ☐ Look good?
- ☐ Feel good?
- ☐ Read well?

8
Application forms

Do not be disheartened if your carefully prepared CV and covering letter results only in an application form. Remember that your CV has achieved something in that the company feel you are worth including in the first stage of the selection process.

From an employer's point of view, application forms put the candidates on an equal footing. Every candidate has to give the information in a similar pattern, and then there is the 'tie-breaker' – questions like: 'How would you describe yourself as a person?'; 'What are your strongest qualities?'; or, 'Why do you want to work for this company?'

It is important to be honest in CVs and covering letters, but perhaps most of all in application forms. Many companies use the application form as part of the contract, and if you have coloured the truth or lied, you could find yourself in real trouble.

Preparing your answers

Always use black ink for ease of photocopying, and write using a pen you are comfortable with. If you can, type your responses unless you are specifically told to write. Before you write anything, photocopy the form and fill in the copy first as practice. You need to be sure that you can fit in everything you want to say, and can edit your answers if necessary to make sure that it is the most relevant and important information that gets prominence.

If you have unlined boxes to complete, put some ruled paper underneath so that you can write in straight lines. Writing that rises or falls will always look untidy.

Read each question carefully and thoroughly, and identify what the company is trying to gain by asking it. Read through the whole form before you begin, and note what information you should put in each section. If you are asked to demonstrate specific skills, e.g., leadership or problem-solving, you will need to think of examples for each rather than use one example in which you led and solved the problems!

It is vital to answer each question, not just give the information you want to give, irrespective of the employer's request. However, with forethought you can usually cover the facts that you want the employer to know.

Do not answer questions by referring the reader back to your CV. You must repeat the information on the form. Make sure you do so in the order and style instructed, not simply by copying it from your CV. After all, employers want someone who can follow simple instructions!

Where not instructed otherwise, fill in sections as you would on a CV: highest qualifications first, most recent employment first, and so on.

Generally, it is the 'Tell us about yourself . . .' questions that are the hardest to answer. These include questions like:

- What are your personal strengths and weaknesses?
- What has been your greatest achievement to date?
- Please give your reasons for applying for *this* post.

The best way to approach these is to discuss them with a friend. Look at all aspects of your work and decide which of the desired skills and attributes you can demonstrate (hopefully most, if not all, of them). Do not worry about how good your examples are; concentrate on getting a good selection, if possible two or three choices for each area, before you think about which to use.

Aim to get a variety of examples so that you can use different ones in different sections. You can often give a different slant to the work you have done so that each example can be used where it suits you best.

For example, if you handled the administration for the move of your department from one floor to another, you could cite this as evidence of your:

- planning abilities (e.g., people placed in offices, computers and telephone lines, secretaries near their managers, etc.);
- interpersonal skills (the need to communicate with staff at all levels, suppliers, etc.);
- administration skills;
- problem-solving (there would be at least one with an office move!).

It would be preferable to use the example of the office move to answer only one question, i.e., to demonstrate your planning abilities. If you were also asked for evidence of interpersonal skills, try to choose a different example. This way you give a good impression of broad experience and can show yourself in a good light in each area. It does, however, take advance planning to use the best example for each question.

When you have decided what will show you in the best light, start putting it into 'professional' words.

If you have to mix good and bad in a question (e.g., 'What are your strongest areas, and also your weakest?'), give most of the good points first, then a recognition of your weaknesses, finishing with another strength; preferably one which relates to and/or counteracts the weakness.

Draft out your response to each of the questions until you are satisfied that you are concise, grammatically correct, showing yourself in the best light *and* can fit your answer into the space allowed.

Completing the form

You will not find questions of the sort below on all application forms. Some are only concerned with basic facts, while others can make you feel that you are being asked to psychologically analyse yourself. However, read through them all – they may trigger inspiration and will almost certainly be good preparation for an interview!

First and foremost, always obey instructions. These usually relate to use of black ink, block capitals, etc.

Name, address, telephone

Give your full name, underlining the name you are known by if it is not your first. Show your title (Dr, Mr, Mrs, Ms, Miss), or complete the box that asks for it. Write your address out in full, including postcode; if you get the job, it may well be used for administrative purposes. Give an STD code for any telephone number, and make any restrictions clear, e.g., 'evenings only', 'use to make appointment only', or, 'for messages'.

Age/date of birth

It is generally better to give these because to omit them makes it look as though you have something to hide, and an employer faced with a pile of CVs does not have time to seek.

Country of birth, nationality/citizenship

As with age, it is better to complete these. If your surname suggests that you might not be a native, you can make a note explaining how many years you have lived in the country if you wish.

Secondary education

As with the CV, give the name and location of the school and the years you attended. There is no need to mention examinations you failed or number of attempts unless you are specifically asked to. There is usually a column for grades, and unless they were years ago (when you genuinely may not be able to remember them), you should put these in because omission gives the appearance of bad grades. Decide whether to put your examination results in order of grade achieved or relevance to the job you are applying for.

Further education

This is sometimes grouped with secondary education. Again, list your examination passes with the most relevant ones first. Give the title of any degree you have achieved, and list the options and subsidiary subjects you have taken; again, most relevant first.

Employment history

This will basically be the same as your CV, although it may need to be abbreviated to fit into the space available. In this case, you should complete all the sections, but refer the reader to your attached CV for further information as well. See the relevant sections earlier in the book.

Anything of relevance?

This question appears in different guises on application forms. If you are leaving school, college, or university, employers are usually looking for examples of your experience of the 'real' world, and on graduate recruitment scheme forms for things that mark you out as having management potential. If you are older and are or have been employed, find something you will bring to the work, but that is not covered in other sections. This may be something you have gained from outside employment or outside your normal duties at work (e.g., running or playing for a staff sports team, if you can use this to demonstrate a skill that is not otherwise obvious within your work). Consider everything you have done with a view to demonstrating any of the following skills:

leadership
communication
working with a team
taking individual responsibility
problem-solving
information analysis
budgeting
negotiation

Examples of this include:

> 'I have been a member of the Hatherton Drama Society, and in 1992 was elected to the post of publicity secretary. I was individually responsible for all aspects of publicity, which involved liaising with directing staff to define the most suitable publicity for each production and the issuing of press releases, etc. I also arranged interviews for the lead players and represented the club at various events.'

> 'I spent several vacations working as voluntary care assistant at a residential home for young people with learning difficulties. In addition to spending time with the residents working within the care plans laid down by the full-time staff, I arranged a series of garden teas to raise funds. This involved liaising with gardening societies, WI, local craft groups etc., to arrange a selection of stalls for each event, advertising, and general administration. The opening of the home achieved a wider understanding of the needs

and abilities of the residents, and raised a total of £1250 to enable a series of day trips.'

'I have played for the company cricket team for six summers and have organized a series of matches with local companies. This has had a positive effect on team spirit within the company, and our place in the top three in the town tournament was a boost in difficult recessionary times.'

Interests/hobbies

As with your CV, try to show a balanced use of your spare time. Never lie – your interviewer may be an avid fan!

Finally, remember that the others applying for the job will almost certainly find the questions as hard as you do – and may not have the benefit of having read this book!

Checklist

Have you:

- ☐ Answered all the questions?
- ☐ Actually answered them, i.e., given the information the employer is looking for?
- ☐ Used different examples in different answers?

9
The covering letter

Although you may have no choice but to send a standard CV for similar jobs, the covering letter must be written separately for each application. You should never send a CV without a covering letter. It is your chance to bring the facts in your CV to life, to make them specifically relevant to the company, and to show something of your personality.

Your CV is a simple record of your qualifications and your experience in a fairly standardized style. The covering letter is your chance to show how that experience makes you the ideal person for the job being advertised.

Despite this, the covering letter should not be more than one A4 page, and the page should not be crammed with typing. It is preferable to give a few salient facts that the employer will read than to include everything and have the important points lost in the chaos.

Opinions differ as to whether or not you should handwrite your letter. If you are asked specifically to write it, of course you must. From one point of view, a handwritten letter is preferable because your handwriting says much about you (hopefully positive!) If your writing is clear and attractive, then write it, using dark-blue or black ink for ease of photocopying. You should always write it out in draft first so that you can check it for length and for any places where the length of the words leaves an unsightly gap on a line. Use plain paper of the same size as for your CV, but with a lined sheet underneath so that you do not wander up or down the page.

The two major disadvantages of handwriting are tidiness or appearance if your writing is less than attractive, and the fact that your letter will take up more paper and you may have to give less information to avoid sending in too many sheets.

If you decide to type, do not do so with full 'justification' (like the printed pages of this book). Although neat, it looks impersonal and an uneven right-hand margin is easier on the eye. Do not be tempted to add extra information to fill the page.

Better to have three positive paragraphs that 'sell' you, than a closely typed page that the employer will not have time to read through.

The basics

Make sure that your **name and address** is clearly shown at the top of the letter, together with a **telephone number**, if you can be rung. Do not think that because this information is on your CV it is not necessary to put it on the letter – even staples fail, and in any event you want to make it as easy for an employer to contact you as you can.

Date the letter with the day on which you send it, and address it to **the person named** in the advertisement. If there is a job title, but no name given, it is well worth ringing the company to ask for the name of the holder of that job so that you can address it personally. Make sure that you get the correct spelling of the name and the initials. If you are writing to a female, you should also find out whether you should address them as Mrs, Miss, or Ms.

There are some companies whose policy is not to give out names over the telephone. The receptionist may be sympathetic if you explain why you want to know, but if they will not tell you, at least find out whether they are male or female so that you can avoid the impersonal 'Dear Sir or Madam' and opt for one or the other.

If you address the letter to a named individual, **sign off** with 'Yours sincerely'. If it is to 'Dear Sir' or 'Dear Madam', end with 'Yours faithfully'.

Make sure that you **head the letter** with the job title and/or reference number of the post that you are applying for. A company may advertise several posts at once, and you need to make sure your CV gets in the right pile.

Some examples of various layout styles are shown below:

THOMAS JACKSON
5 Beech Close
Endmore
Gloucestershire

Work: (0123) 456789

Mr A. J. Dark
Bishop & Sons
14 High Street
Gloucester

23 March 1994

Dear Mr Dark

Post of 'Accounts Clerk'

I would like to apply for the above post, advertised in this week's edition of 'The Star' . . .

THOMAS JACKSON
5 Beech Close, Endmore, Gloucestershire
(0123) 456789

Mr A. J. Dark
Bishop & Sons
14 High Street
Gloucester

23 March 1994

Dear Mr Dark

Re: Post of 'Accounts Clerk'

I would like to apply for the above post, advertised in this week's edition of 'The Star' . . .

Read and reread your letter, preferably aloud, to make sure that it **reads smoothly**, and finally look at it to make sure that it is appealing to the eye, even before it is read.

Selling yourself

As part of writing your CV, you should have identified the knowledge, skills, and attributes required for the post you want and made sure that you have demonstrated your relevant skills and experience in the CV. You should use your covering letter to draw the employer's attention to your most *relevant* qualifications or experience. You will probably not have room to do this for every one, so it is essential to pick out the most important (first choice), *or* the areas where you most exactly match the requirements (second choice).

Personalize your letter

Another possibility is using research to find out something specific to the company and start with this in your letter. For example:

> 'I see that you are building a new warehouse in East Langley and . . .'

> 'I read in the local business news that you have appointed the general manager to head your IT Support Department and intend to lead the field within three years. I was particularly interested in the advertisement in 'The Standard' for telephone support staff because . . .'

This approach is certainly not suitable for every letter, but particularly for speculative letters, can add that little something that gets your CV read.

Be positive and specific

Make sure that the tone of your letter is positive. Avoid vague phrases like, 'I wish to apply for . . .', or, 'I hope to hear from you . . .' Employers do not generally want wishers and hopers, preferring more positive people.

Avoid general statements such as 'able to work on own

initiative', or, 'enjoys working with people'. If these attributes are shown to be required by the advertisement, demonstrate that you have them with evidence, rather than making the bald statement.

End the letter on a positive note, asking for an interview, but obliquely with phrases like, 'I look forward to hearing from you', or 'I would like to be considered for this post, and look forward to receiving an application form.'

Speculative letters

These are the letters that accompany your CV when you send it to a company without their advertising a post. The idea is that you may catch their interest and be put on file for future vacancies, or that a post may be coming up and you might be suitable to fill it without the time and expense involved in recruiting through advertising.

Be clear about your objective with a speculative letter. The usual covering letter will be aimed to secure you an interview, whereas the speculative letter should result in your name being put in an active file for future recruitment. Occasionally, you may be called in for a general interview even if there is not a specific post, but you will be disappointed if you expect this to happen as the norm.

You will need to ring the company to find out the name and job title of the person you should contact, and address the letter to them personally. Because no specific vacancy exists (that you know of) you cannot tailor your letter to show your suitability. In this case you should identify your most valuable strengths (in terms of knowledge, skills and attributes) and demonstrate these, relating them to the business and style of the company.

Ideally the letter will be four paragraphs long:

1. An introductory paragraph asking about employment. If you have been referred by someone, mention their name briefly provided they have enough clout to be impressive.

2. A clear explanation of what you are looking for (the type of employment, not the salary and holiday entitlement).

3 An outline of your knowledge, skills, and attributes and how these will benefit the company – only a couple of examples!

4 An offer to give any further information required, and a positive close.

Make sure that you keep a copy of every letter you send. If you get called for an interview, you will need to know what you have already said.

MARTIN SANGER
The Cottage, 4 Oddpiece, Amford, Warburton, Lincs
0987 654321 (work)

The Personnel Officer
Armstrong & Hatching
Unit 24
Silver Street Industrial Centre
Warburton
Lincs

29 May 1994

Dear Sir,

Garage Manager, Ref: AG157

I am writing in response to your advertisement on the local radio 'Jobshop' for a garage manager.

I come from a family of car enthusiasts and joined a local garage at 17 to serve my apprenticeship. During this time I received two awards, one for mechanical ability and one for best student. After five years, I moved on to become lead mechanic with Petersons, and became assistant workshop manager shortly afterwards, which involved the scheduling of work and general administration in addition to specialized mechanical work and some routine servicing . . .

Jackie Forbes
Flat 24, 105 London Road
Alderton, Gloucestershire

2 April 1994

Mr P. Jenkins
Wizz Music Store
Shepton Town High Street
Northampton

Dear Mr Jenkins

Post of store manager

As a long-time customer of your store in Milton Keynes, I was interested to see your advertisement for a store manager.

I am currently assistant manager of three branches of SportsPro, a chain of sports and leisure shops which covers the South East, with a young and active customer base. I regularly stand in for the manager in any of these stores for periods of up to two weeks, with full responsibility for decisions relating to customers' problems and other day-to-day concerns . . .

Checklist

Have you:

- ☐ Demonstrated that your experience is relevant to the needs of the employer?
- ☐ Used A4 paper and typed your letter (or used dark-blue or black ink)?
- ☐ Given your name, address, and telephone number?
- ☐ Addressed it to a named person, with correct spelling?
- ☐ Checked the letter for spelling, grammar, and general layout?

Index